7 Destructive

Economic

Illusions

Conquered

Robert Meyer

Dedicated to my dear friend George Burks, who helped me conquer my economic illusions. Was it really that long ago?

Table of Contents
Part 1 – 7 Economic Illusions Conquered

Table of Contents
Part 2 – Conquering More Economic Illusions

Part 1

7 Destructive

Economic

Illusions

Conquered

Introduction

Economic illusions are running amuck. Sound economic reasoning seems difficult to come by. Is it any wonder that our so-called economic recovery favors only certain sectors of the economy.

Wouldn't it be amazing if you could spot the difference between economic illusion and economic reality? Wouldn't it be even more amazing if you gained enough knowledge to protect you and your loved ones from the wealth destruction that ruins the lives of many innocent victims? Wouldn't it be liberating not having to rely on establishment "experts" for financial advice?

Imagine what it would be like for you to escape from the economic illusions that permeate the lives of most people.

As you read every word of this report, you will be stunned at what I reveal. Here they are: 7 economic illusions that reap havoc on our already fragile economy and unfortunately on your future prospects for success, prosperity and happiness.

However, don't despair. You will soon possess the key to free yourself from the prison of economic illusions. You will conquer the illusions.

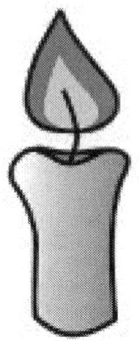

Illusion #1

The Government

Creates Wealth

Illusion #1

The Government Creates Wealth

Reality: The government doesn't create wealth—it redistributes it through inflation and taxation. To the superficial observer, the government appears altruistic when it buys mortgages and injects capital into banks to alleviate the hardships of homeowners and irresponsible bankers.

As I have stated on many occasions, social altruism amounts to nothing but theft, the transfer of wealth from productive to non-productive citizens. **When government bails the undeserved out of trouble, it does so at the expense of innocent people.**

The economist Dr. Arthur Laffer, famous for his "Laffer Curve" concerning rates of taxation, states that every $100 billion in bailout money requires at least $130 billion in taxes. You may be asking "Where does the other $30 billion go?" It is the cost for getting the government involved. In other words, it goes into the pockets of government bureaucrats. $130 billion is transferred from taxpayers into the bottomless pits of the government and special interest groups. We should relegate the "government creating wealth" myth to the same place as the "Tooth Fairy, Easter Bunny and Santa Claus" myths.

Okay, you're probably wondering how you can protect yourself from this obvious rip-off of the taxpayers.

I don't believe there is much you can do to change the political system, except for uncompromisingly supporting the free enterprise system. However, you can be the type of person who practices the virtues of self-reliance and self-responsibility. You probably know that you and only you can create the wealth you desire.

Under the free enterprise system, what's left of it, you create wealth by satisfying the consumers' most urgent desires. You trade value for value. You offer people goods and services they rate high on their scale of values. In return, they pay you for these goods and services.

If you are already earning good money, then conquering economic illusions will definitely help you retain your wealth, which makes it easier for you to accumulate more of it.

If you are seeking a profitable niche, look at the hobbies or activities that stimulate your desire and passion. You may be surprised to discover one of these contains a golden key to success.

You are intelligent enough to realize the government has no more ability to create wealth than a dog has the ability to sprout wings and fly to the moon. Unfortunately, government does possess the means to destroy wealth at a quickened pace.

What can we conclude? Obviously, you must protect yourself from that gargantuan machine of wealth destruction, the government.

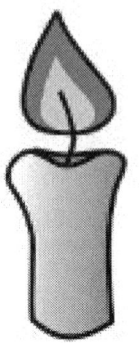

Illusion #2

This Time it is

Different

Illusion #2

This Time it is Different

The political and financial establishment convinced people "The New Economics" guaranteed prosperity and abundance for all.

Reality: "The New Economics" represent a gross violation of sound economic reasoning. It is actually a rehash of the faulty economics that great economists such as Ludwig von Mises, Murray Rothbard, F. A. Hayek and Henry Hazlitt exploded many times over.

Consider this: Bad economics will eventually sink any economy no matter how much people believe that this time it is different. Praxeology (the science of human action) is the real economics—you know, the Real McCoy of sound economic reasoning. Certainly, its laws are eternal and unchanging. As long as the human race possesses the same logical structure of mind, that is, it possesses a human brain, the laws of praxeology remain valid for eternity.

Politicians, altruists, do-gooders and world-improvers convinced the masses that anything goes in the arena of economic policy. Their blatant disregard of Economic Law guarantees our economy continues to sink into the abyss of economic collapse, or at best economic stagnation. Sometimes it seems as if we are experiencing a recovery. However, this is only a short-term interruption of the long-term trend.

Many people become desperate for solutions to problems that come their way unbidden. This opens the door for crooks and charlatans to prey on them with quack economic solutions, convincing their victims that faulty economics supply the means to abundance and prosperity for all.

Notice how the financial and political establishment uses terms such as positive change, stimulating the economy, creating jobs, saving jobs, too big to fail and easy credit with reckless abandon. Let me ask you. Are they actually making concrete statements? Is it possible that each of these phrases is nothing but a floating abstraction, taken out of context?

Politicians and their friends in the news media love to feed you

myths and illusions. In fact, what they are indulging in amounts to doublespeak.

Here's what their "misleading" terms produce in reality.

1. Positive change = negative change
2. Stimulating the economy = inflation and reduction of wealth
3. Creating jobs = eliminating jobs
4. Saving jobs = eliminating new employment opportunities
5. To big to fail = penalizing profitable business, preventing new business creation
6. Easy credit = more debt and malinvestments
7. Beneficial regulations = more restrictions on your personal liberty and freedom

How would you like to predict the consequences of economic policy at least 90% of the time? Here's how you accomplish this marvelous feat.

When a politician or establishment economist claims a certain policy will produce a certain result use contrary reasoning. Believe it will produce the opposite result. You'll amaze everyone with your phenomenal success rate.

Circumstances may change, but Economic Law remains valid through eternity. Now let's move on to conquering more illusions.

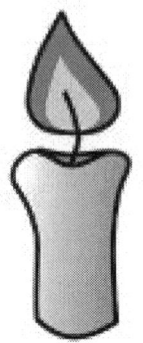

Illusion #3

Government

Interventionism

Helps Marketplace

Illusion #3

Government Interventionism Helps Marketplace

Reality: All government interventions on the marketplace violate Economic Law and only worsen the situation.

Here's the chain of events in the life of a government intervention.

Altruists, world-improvers and do-gooders spot something on the marketplace that isn't working according to their spurious definition of morality and justice. They claim to have discovered another instance of the failure of capitalism. Of course, the only solution that occurs to their limited power of reason is interfering in order to "improve" the situation. In their role as politician or bureaucrat, they pass a law or create another regulation. This is the beginning of their efforts to turn a mole hole into an unscalable mountain.

As to be expected, sometime in the future they discover the situation has worsened, never stopping to consider that their original intervention caused the new undesirable result. So what does a limited thinker or greedy politician do? Pass another law or create another regulation without thinking about the consequences.

Of course, the situation continues to deteriorate. Instead of checking their premises and discovering where things when wrong, our "beloved" leaders saddle the economy with new laws or regulations, hammering another nail in the coffin of economic progress. **(Note: Driven by their sick desire to achieve complete totalitarianism, some intellectuals and power mongers actually attempt to destroy the free enterprise system.)**

Now imagine thousands upon thousands of laws and regulations foisted on the marketplace. Is it any wonder our economy continues to decline? Eventually, the cost of all the interference on the marketplace becomes prohibitive. Members of the political and financial establishment seem intent on permanently sabotaging our already fragile economy.

Now here's something that could make your blood boil. How do the interventionists respond? They have the gall to blame Laissez faire capitalism for our economic problems, problems they created. Are these people plain stupid, or just downright dishonest?

Here' a question you should ask. Who are the true culprits of implacable conflict in society? Well, here's the answer. Altruists, do-gooders, world-improvers, politicians and bureaucrats create disharmony and chaos in our society by wielding the heavy-hand of government interventionism. If left to its own devices, the marketplace, under a social system of Laissez faire (unhampered) capitalism, creates as much mutual harmony as possible in the sphere of human action.

Government interventionism on the marketplace is doomed to failure. It cannot achieve the desired ends. It can only further aggravate the situation. Individuals acting in their own interest are quite capable of making decisions without any "help" from the government. I'm sure you realize that as a unique individual, you stand closer to the events of your life than anyone else does.

Does another person know what you need and desire more than you do? Isn't it ridiculous to believe that a politician or a bureaucrat has the knowledge to decide what you require for your existence? From all the political scandals we hear about, we can assume that they cannot take care of their own needs honestly and efficiently. I think we can conclude that it's the height of absurdity to think politicians and bureaucrats can make wise decisions for millions of individuals.

Let's accept a timeless truth. Governments possess absolutely no means to help the marketplace. However, they do possess the weapons to cause market annihilation.

Here's the way it is. **Government has only one legitimate function, to protect an individual's life, liberty and property. Any government interference with voluntary exchanges violates these sacred rights —and is therefore criminal.**

You are probably asking what you should do about this undesirable state of affairs. Here's a solution. Understand that when the government interferes with voluntary exchanges, it destroys values by forcing people to be satisfied with goods and services lower on their scale of values. It diminishes human satisfaction.

With your newly acquired knowledge, you won't allow politicians and their cronies in the news media to trick you into believing that another law, regulation or intervention benefits you. Happily, you'll bet your money on an outcome contrary to what they claim they'll achieve.

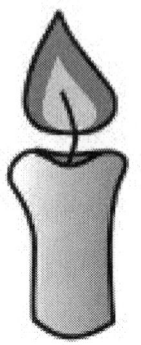

Illusion #4

Fed Benefits

Economy with Low

Interest Rates

Illusion #4

Fed Benefits Economy with Low Interest Rates

Reality: The market rate of interest consists of three components that correspond to the actual state of reality.

The three components are:
1.   Time Component
2.   Risk Component
3.   Inflation Component (Inflation Premium)

By the time, you finish reading this section, you'll wonder how our political and financial leaders could possibly justify manipulating interest rates.

Federal Reserve manipulation of interest rates causes boom and bust cycles because it gives investors and entrepreneurs false signals—resulting in them diverting production from the consumers' most urgent desires into areas of production that cannot be sustained.

Here's a short, concise explanation. The rate of interest manifests as a market phenomenon that corresponds to reality.

First of all, the time component gives information on how people weigh the future against the present. If they prefer to delay consumption and save for the future, the rate of interest tends to fall. If they prefer immediate consumption at the expense of future savings, the rate tends to rise.

Leave it to politicians and inflationary bankers to attempt to eliminate the reality of time.

The risk component is just that—how risky a loan is. The riskier the loan is, the higher the rate of interest. A relatively safe loan tends to have a low or negligible rate of interest included in its final rate.

Obviously, the only risk politicians accept, is that you lose your money through inflation and taxation.

15

An inflation premium is included if lenders and borrowers expect prices to rise. The more they expect prices to increase, the higher the rate of interest. The final rate includes all three components.

Politicians love inflationary money because they can pay off their cronies and favorite sons with it. Plus, members of the elite gain the advantage of purchasing goods and services before prices have increased. The real kick in the teeth for taxpayers happens when inflation rears its ugly head and knocks down their standard of living with higher prices.

As you can see, Fed policy of lowering the rate of interest to practically 0% is absurd. Unbelievably, Fed members blatantly ignore sound monetary theory by claiming:

1. People no longer wish to consume anything today, delaying all consumption until sometime in the future. **Fact:** This is ridiculous. If people actually eliminated all consumption of goods and services, the human race would perish.
2. There no longer exists any risk in extending loans to businesses and individuals. **Fact:** Talk about the height of absurdity; Federal Reserve easy money policies resulted in excessive debts that many debtors can never repay.
3. Inflation is past history. **Fact:** It looks as if bad economics will be our past, present and future. Price increases might seem tame now; however, by time our government completes its "evil inflationary mission" Atlas will have shrugged, causing production to come to an almost complete standstill. **The result:** Many goods and services will quickly vanish from the marketplace resulting in massive shortages of what people need and desire.

Consider this: One solution to our economic woes is to allow the rate of interest to increase to its natural level. The natural interest rate would wash all malinvestments out of the marketplace—resulting in producers satisfying the most urgent desires of productive citizens. We must abolish the onerous Federal Reserve System, forever stopping its policy of creating monetary mayhem.

You may be wondering what you can do to protect yourself. Well, if inflationary money causes the price of goods and services to soar, you certainly don't want to be left holding the bag. The day may come when your grocery bag holds only worthless paper dollars—that is if we don't suffer a deflationary collapse.

Thank God, I'm not a licensed, establishment investment adviser. Therefore, I'm not dispensing investment advice. Instead, I'll ask you some questions. What does the newly learned knowledge tell you? What kind of commodities have people valued since the beginning of time? What does the best jewelry consist of?

Because of the chance for a slow, syrupy decline of the dollar or even a deflation, I am asking the most important question of all. What is it you value most?

Here's some important advice. Allow money to circulate in your life. Spend it on goods and services that supply you the greatest long-term satisfaction. Also, learn the value of capital accumulation. Spend less than you earn.

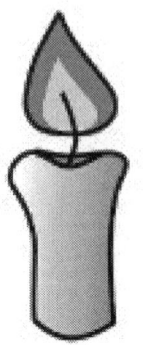

Illusion #5

Flaws of Capitalism

Cause Recessions -

Depressions

Illusion #5

Flaws of Capitalism Cause Recessions - Depressions

Reality #1 Government interventionism completely disrupts the smooth functioning of the marketplace resulting in permanent economic decline.

Reality #2 Federal Reserve policy of artificially lowering interest rates and increasing the money supply to "stimulate" the economy causes boom and bust cycles resulting in economic recessions and depressions.

The dishonesty of politicians knows no bounds. Lie, cheat and steal reigns supreme as the rule of the political game. By blaming capitalism for causing economic crisis, they engage in what I call the **"BIG LIE"** Unless our "beloved" leaders are intellectually dishonest or just plain ignorant, they know damn well their own destructive policies cause our economic woes.

Happily for you, it's time to expose their incredibly weak and fallacious economic theories.

The war of many illusions continues—and one of the illusions concerns an erroneous belief about the ravaging, but unacknowledged corrective force of deflation. "Economists" declare that our political and financial leaders make an all out effort to eradicate that demon known as deflation. These pseudo-economists tell us that falling prices are the equivalent of a depression that will make the 30's look innocuous in comparison. On the advice of these so-called experts of economic analysis, the government along with Federal Reserve System embarked on humongous bailout maneuvers to save us from this deadly enemy of prosperity and well-being.

It's amazing that only a few people questioned and analyzed the economic "wisdom" of our political and financial leaders. For it is certainly flawed. In order to understand deflation, it is necessary that we define the term.

Classical Definition of Deflation

Deflation is a decrease in the quantity of money (money supply) which results in a rise in the purchasing power of the monetary unit. In other words, each dollar, euro, yen, etc. possesses more purchasing power. An unfortunate consequence of deflation is that it falsifies economic calculation and impairs the ability of capitalists and entrepreneurs to appraise profits and losses. The larger the decrease in the quantity of money, the more it disarranges consumption, investment and production. It benefits some at the expense of others. Deflation is seldom a policy governments purposely embark upon. Inflation remains their favorite method of manipulating the currency for the benefit of special interests.

Classical Definition of Inflation

Inflation is an increase in the quantity of money (money supply) which results in a drop in the purchasing power of the monetary unit. You receive less for your money. As with deflation, economic calculation is impaired, diminishing the ability of entrepreneurs and capitalists to appraise profits and losses. The larger the increase in the quantity of money, the more it disturbs consumption, investment and production patterns. Inflationary money often tricks entrepreneurs and capitalists into embarking on ventures that the marketplace eventually exposes as malinvestments.

What makes inflation so insidious, is that it benefits the people who first receive the inflationary money. They gain the advantage of purchasing what they need at current prices. As the money, moves through the economic system, it causes overall prices to rise, although it doesn't affect the various goods and services the same. Some prices rise faster than others do. A few may not rise at all due to declining demand.

Now here's where inflation victimizes innocent people. The unfortunate individuals at the end of the line end up paying higher prices. The thrifty individual who attempts to accumulate capital by saving his money soon discovers his purchasing power has decreased.

The hapless citizen living on a fixed income suffers a lower standard of living.

Let's put it like this. Unless you and I have political connections, we end up holding the short end of the stick. Think about it. Has the Fed sent you a letter notifying you about all the great benefits you will receive from the newly created money?

Current Definition of Deflation and Inflation – Tricks of the Political and Financial Establishment

The ascendancy of faulty economics resulted in establishment economists reversing cause and effect. They now define deflation as falling prices and inflation as prices rising. These are effects—the results of deflation and inflation. Remember deflation is a decrease in the quantity of money. Inflation is an increase in the quantity of money. Of course, these days most people accept the faulty definitions.

You may be wondering why they would reverse cause and effect. If you ask the following questions, you'll know why the establishment prefers that you believe in illusions.

Here are the questions—and answers that will probably annoy you. Who controls our money? The Federal Reserve System. Who directs the flow of the newly created money? The government and the Federal Reserve System. Our government and the onerous Federal Reserve System work together to make sure the "right people" receive the inflationary money. I probably don't have to tell you that the political and financial establishment doesn't consider us as the "right people."

By the way, a social system of unhampered capitalism with its monetary system of 100% gold-backing guarantees continually declining prices—benefiting both consumers and producers. The consumers' standard of living soars and producers earn greater profits by offering more goods and services.

How perverted! Consumers and taxpayers reap earned benefits instead of the political and financial establishment extorting unearned benefits. Heaven forbid! Anyway, you now know why the political and financial establishment hates the Gold Standard.

The Cause of Our Economic Woes

You probably never imagined how far the treachery of the establishment could go. The reason why its members want you to believe the faulty definitions of deflation and inflation is so they can divert blame from the creators of our economic woes to some imagined "culprits. Who do our perpetrators of economic mayhem place the blame on? Well the scapegoats are "greedy" capitalists, speculators, short-sellers, consumers spending too little, consumers spending too much, people saving too much money, people not saving enough money, ad infinitum.

Here's another question you can ask. Since the Federal Reserve System controls our currency and along with the government determines where the newly created money goes, who is responsible for our current economic woes? Certainly, I don't have to answer that question.

The Boom Cycle

As I explained in the section on the classical definition of inflation, increases in the quantity of money cause economic distortions. During the past 25 years, we've been "blessed" with considerable increases that resulted in the tech boom, the stock market boom and the housing boom. When Alan Greenspan lowered the Federal Funds rate to practically nothing (to counterbalance the effects of the tech collapse), he guaranteed there would be an unsustainable boom somewhere in the economy. Conditions dictated that much of the inflationary money found its way into the housing market. Illusions are just that—illusions. Right now, it appears that economic illusions are in abundance. Let's face it. All artificial booms end in busts.

The Bust Cycle

Allow yourself to imagine a scene—a scene of total disarray where the wild party of excess has come to a crashing end. The partygoers wantonly consumed all the booze and drugs of false prosperity. Now comes the time of hangovers and drug withdrawals. The addicts of inflationary money must go into rehab. The recovery will prove to be long and painful—that is if the government allows a recovery.

Unfortunately, our government and the Federal Reserve System continues their futile attempt to keep the party going with massive injections of inflationary money. It is all in vain. Lenders won't lend money to people who can't and won't pay them back. Many debtors borrowed themselves into a deep hole. Of course, it is possible that the newly created money could cause a hyperinflationary boom—with the tragic result of goods and services disappearing from the marketplace. It definitely won't stimulate the production of needed goods and services.

Trillions of dollars "vanished" from the world economy. What happened to it? The money didn't exist in the first place. It was phony Federal Reserve money—a money illusion. Individuals were relying on paper money and bank credits that didn't actually exist.

Bill Bonner of "The Daily Reckoning" calls the marketplace "Mr. Market." Well, Mr. Market has exposed it all as a fraud. Now he is attempting to restore wealth to its rightful owners—those productive individuals who produce value and those thrifty people who save money. **That is precisely what a recession or depression accomplishes; it restores wealth to the producers of wealth.**

What should you do about all of this? You need to place yourself in the position of one of the rightful owners of wealth.

Now that you know what's happening, let's determine what the government should do about our continuing economic woes, using the wisdom of one of the greatest thinkers of the 20th century.

When someone asked the great economist Ludwig von Mises what the government should do about the depression (the depression of the 30's) he said "nothing—a lot sooner."

I'm sure you realize governments never follow sound economic principles. Instead, they tamper with the marketplace, hampering its efficiency and destroying its smooth functioning. The massive bailouts (QQE—Quack Quantitative Easing) will prove deadly to our economy and the future of the dollar. Here's a scary scenario. It is possible the inflationary money could transform the continuing economic decline into a hyperinflationary collapse, turning the dollar into "toilet paper" currency and destroying our economy. Of course, it is possible we suffer a slow, painful decline.

Ludwig von Mises also observed "Government is the only entity that can take a perfectly useful commodity like paper, and turn it into something that is completely worthless."

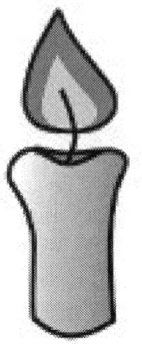

Illusion #6

The Government

Creates Jobs

Illusion #6

The Government Creates Jobs

Reality: Government completely lacks the ability to create jobs; however, it definitely possesses the weapons of job elimination.

You've probably noticed the majority of people actually believe the government creates jobs. Apparently, the unwary accept this myth without thinking it through, never questioning where the government receives the funds to begin its job creation program.

Now let's conquer another illusion!

You decide you want to create a start-up business. Certainly, you need capital. Either you saved up the funds or you must borrow them. In addition, it is possible to receive some of the start-up capital from investors who see the possibility of profiting from your venture.

Now assume the government claims it is creating 5 million jobs. Now ask "Where does it get the capital for its job creation scheme?" Obviously, it isn't using accumulated savings. Gee, in your wildest dreams, can you imagine the government saving money instead of running deficits? The truth is that government cannot create wealth. So, where does it find the money to fund any project?

Governmental Methods of Raising Capital

Basically, governments have only three methods to acquire the capital needed to "create" jobs.

1. They raise it through taxation.
2. They create money out of thin air.
3. They sell bonds and other assets on the open market.

Now let these insights sink in for a moment. It should be evident the government method of raising capital siphons it from the marketplace. If it raises capital through taxation, it diminishes the taxpayers' ability to consume goods and services, and decreases their ability to save money.

Guess what? **Economic improvement requires more savings and investment per capita, the only method of job and wealth creation.**

As discussed in Illusions #4 and #5, when the government through the Federal Reserve System, inflates the money supply it causes artificial booms. All artificial booms divert production from the consumers' most urgent desires into projects that rank lower on their scale of values. In other word, inflation fosters malinvestments—projects that can't be sustained. The boom suddenly transforms into a bust, causing widespread unemployment—as you can obviously see.

Inflation also devalues the purchasing power of the currency. For you, this means the money you saved is worth less. Less savings and investment per capita means a prosperity reduction, resulting in the job creation process slowing down.

Now consider this sad fact. When the government sells bonds and other assets on the open market it removes money from the marketplace. The result: It diverts savings from profitable free enterprise ventures into government coffers, a tragedy that is occurring as investors seek "safety" in government T-Bills (Treasury Bills). It's sad when people seek comfort from government vehicles of "wealth."

A Secondary Consequence

Let's go to the extreme and assume the government can invest each dollar as efficiently as entrepreneurs and capitalists. You're intelligent enough to know this sounds far-fetched. Anyway, what do you think? Would it then be even-steven? Is it possible that it doesn't matter if the government or the free enterprise system creates jobs?

Obviously, bureaucratic endeavors are expensive and wasteful because bureaucracies do not operate by profit and loss. They operate by bureaucratic rules and regulations. Business operates by the profit motive. If a business satisfies consumer desires efficiently, it earns profits and remains a going concern. Do you know what happens when a producer of goods and services defies consumer desires? Unless he quickly wises up, he suffers losses, goes out business, and is no longer able to waste scarce resources.

Once you figure in the cost of bureaucratic waste, there is actually a net decline in job creation. Government meddling in the job market eliminates more jobs than it creates—and the jobs it does "create" aren't ones desired by consumers.

The Solution

Now it is important for you to meditate on the following solution.

We must permanently remove the government from the "job creation" market. In his masterpiece "Human Action" Ludwig von Mises states "A government can no more determine prices than a goose can lay hen's eggs." I'm sure he would apply the statement to the prospect of government creating jobs. I'm using his words in this context. "The government can no more create jobs than a goose can lay hen's eggs." However, it definitely possesses the means to eliminate jobs—to permanently hamper the market's ability to create employment opportunities for all.

By now, you know all government intervention on the marketplace eliminates jobs. Government created inflation, excess taxes, minimum wage laws, tariffs and so-called socially "beneficial" legislation imposed on employers cause unemployment and actually defies the best interests of the worker.

Laissez faire (unhampered) capitalism remains the only social system that can guarantee jobs for all who desire employment. It's the one that offers you the opportunity to honestly create the wealth and prosperity you desire.

As you keep reading every word of this report you get the feeling all economic principles are interconnected. Your feelings are correct. After all, the universe exists as one vast interconnected energy system. Just imagine the marketplace as a harmonious system satisfying people's desires. So let's put it together, or even better, let's discover how it's all put together.

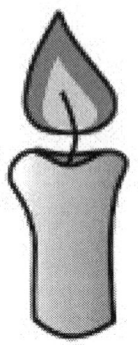

Illusion #7

Economics is not an

Exact Science

Illusion #7

Economics is not an Exact Science

Reality: Regardless of what socialists and government interventionists claim, there is a valid school of economic theory called praxeology, the science of human action.

Allow yourself to relax, open up your mind and concentrate easily on the next surprising statement.

As soon as someone mentions economics, most people, having been misled by the enemies of freedom, envision being subjected to a dry, boring subject. Establishment economists have turned a science based on common sense and easily understood principles into an esoteric hodge-podge of equations, graphs and charts. These economic quacks are determined to stop you from learning anything about this "dismal" subject. As long as people are in the dark, politicians and altruists can make any claim, regardless of proof, allowing them to victimize innocent people, such as you, without opposition. OK, let's reveal something the establishment hopes you never discover.

The truth is: **Economics is exciting. It's about people and their actions, part of the general science of Human Action.** I guarantee the equations, graphs and charts the enemies of liberty use are meaningless. They have nothing to do with individuals and their actions. The real science of economics will supply you with your most effective weapons. Its validity delivers a devastating blow to the political and financial establishment.

Praxeology – The Exciting Science of Human Action

Praxeology is a deductive science that reasons from ultimate principles that are 'a priori.' Of course, since it is the science of human action, its starting point in all analysis of market phenomena is the individual. Now, isn't that something to get excited about! Understand, you are the starting point in all analysis of market phenomena.

Let me remind you that the political establishment hopes you never discover the following information. If enough people embraced it, they would possess the power to end the dishonest careers of this elite group of plunderers.

Praxeology exists as a manifestation of the human mind, dealing with the actions that are open to individuals in achieving their chosen ends. People act—because not to act is non-existence. An individual comes into the world with instincts that may preserve his life, however what separates him from the lower animals is his power of reason. His ability to reason allows him to choose possible courses of action, so that he can act to achieve his goals and desires. The strong-willed, reasoning individual, who acts with purpose, is more likely to achieve success than men and women who are weak-willed or somewhere in between.

Here's an important fact for you to understand. Society cannot act, since it is only a combination of its individuals. Only individuals act. Happily, people can embark on cooperative action to attain common goals.

Praxeology begins its reasoning from an individual action and develops the full implications of that action. As stated in "Mises Made Easier" prepared by Percy L. Greaves Jr. "Praxeology aims at knowledge valid for instances in which the conditions correspond to those implied in its assumptions and inferences. Its statement and propositions are not derived from experience, but are antecedent to any comprehension of historical facts." It is a deductive science.

Obviously, when you take action on something, you start a chain of consequences. Of course, effective actions result in desirable consequences.

Axiomatic Concepts and 'a Priori' Categories

Here's an exercise in futility. Try to envision human life without action—void of individuals attempting to satisfy goals and desires. It is absurd, unthinkable.

Ayn Rand identified three axiomatic concepts.
* Existence
* Identity
* Consciousness

Try to visualize non-existence, non-identity and non-consciousness. Metaphysicians speak about achieving a higher state of consciousness through arriving at a state of non-consciousness. What they actually mean is reaching samadhi, which manifests as an incredibly euphoric state of mind—as I can personally verify. Even though you reach a state of oneness, it is still a conscious state of mind.

I've been meditating for years and never did I reach a state of non-consciousness. Wait a minute! I just experienced a profound insight. I am enlightened. I realize that I exist—and it isn't an illusion. I have identity as a human being, just as you have identity as a human being. You and I absolutely possess consciousness. Without existence, identity and consciousness there would be no me to meditate. I conclude that I exist —I have identity—therefore I am consciousness.

An 'a priori' premise is the starting point of all deductive reasoning, a statement we can't question or contradict. It's impossible for us to trace it back to any prior causes. Now we do not need to begin a discussion of whether Universal Mind, Infinite Intelligence, God or the Big Bang created all there is or is the ultimate cause of all there is. It's irrelevant from a praxeological standpoint.

As far as I can tell, there are six 'a priori' categories of human action. The categories are present in all human actions.

Now stick with me. If you've read this far, you exist as a rare thinking individual.

Causality – Cause and Effect

Cause and effect relationships exist in every action. I'm sure you realize that effective actions raise the possibility of you achieving what you desire. In addition, you know regularity exists in natural phenomena, making it possible for you to plan and act. You certainly couldn't act effectively in a chaotic physical environment.

Time

Every action involves the passing of time. Everything you plan or do takes a certain amount of time. The time span can range anywhere from a second to years. Many of your goals and desires require long-term planning. You must plant seeds and nurture the growth of your ambition, before you harvest the results of your efforts. Many people are too impatient to allow their goals and desires to manifest, which is why patience is a prized virtue.

Uncertainty

Ludwig von Mises states in "Human Action" "The uncertainty of the future is already implied in the very notion of acting." Uncertainty causes extreme neurosis in some people. The neurotic individual lives in constant fear about some unknown happening that may occur. Government interventionism on the marketplace disrupts markets, causing chaotic conditions, increasing the amount of fear and uncertainty people experience.

Change

Just as love is, change is often the maker of despair. An individual can learn to master change by anticipating future conditions more successfully than most—or he can suffer the consequences of becoming a victim of unforeseen changes. Try envisioning non-change, it isn't possible. Non-change is equivalent to non-existence. **Allow change to become your best friend instead of your worst enemy.**

Logic

All human possess the same logical structure of mind. If this weren't so, it would prove impossible to communicate with each other. Have you recently attempted a conversation with a grasshopper or antelope? Unless you're a shaman or warrior of the Carlos Castaneda school of metaphysics, this probably wasn't very productive. Now, I admit the logical structure of one individual may be more efficient than that of another. However, this doesn't invalidate the fact that all humans are endowed with the same logical structure of mind. We were born with human brains.

Value

The theory of subjective value revolutionized the science of economics. Classical economists believed that value was inherent in the goods and services offered on the marketplace, failing to realize value resides in the minds of men. You, as a unique individual, decide what you value and don't value by arranging your values on a scale from highest to lowest. During the day, your scale of values constantly shifts. Once you fulfill one value or desire you immediately attempt to fulfill what is next in line, hoping you receive the maximum satisfaction from your actions.

The "a Priori" Categories in Action

The "a priori" categories are present in all human actions. Every action you embark on involves cause and effect. Each action results in an effect. Each action happens in time. Uncertainty exists in every action, although in many cases the uncertainty is miniscule. The more steps in a course of action or the more complicated the action, the more uncertainty you experience. Of course, every action brings about change and must allow for change. In analyzing any course of action, you reason it out, rely on your intuitive powers, use a combination of both or depend on base instincts. Regardless, your logical structure of mind, your human brain is involved. Certainly, you never make plans and goals and follow a course of action unless it conforms to your scale of values. However, hidden subconscious desires often guide your actions, sometimes in contradiction to your stated goals.

I'm sure you realize that a person can state that he values this more than he values that. He claims he prefers A to B and B to C. However, his actions contradict his statement. He fails to walk the talk. In his behavior, he may display the fact that he prefers C to A or that he prefers D to any of the above. What a man or woman says is irrelevant. His or her actions reveal the true value system.

Praxeology Refutes Faulty Economic Theory

We have placed the establishment economists with their backs to the wall. We have blindfolded them, although you can make a case that they were already blind. The firing squad of logic and reason is ready for action.

Mathematical economists attempt to quantify human action in their equations, which is absurd. There is no way anyone can quantify an individual's value system. You can say the person prefers A to B, but it's impossible to measure the intensity of his preference for A over B. You might love your spouse more than you love your best friend. But can you honestly state you love your spouse 33.3% more than you love your best friend? Definitely not. As you can see, the use of mathematical equations to quantify cause and effect relationships in human action is nonsensical and meaningless.

Equations are quite useful in obtaining knowledge in an inductive science such as classical physics; but useless in discovering knowledge in the deductive sciences of praxeology and logic. Mathematical economists are only fooling themselves when they take a perfectly useful science and misuse it. The deductive science of mathematics efficiently does the job when adding up costs and prices. You know what amazes me and should amaze you? The mathematical economist uses his equations to justify interfering with market processes, obliterating the efficiency of the pricing system.

The praxeologist, the master of human action, realizes all government interference with the market is doomed to failure, He advocates the social system of Laissez faire (unhampered) capitalism, not because of unfounded opinions, but because he realizes the theorems of praxeology are scientific and correspond to the nature of reality. **Praxeology proves beyond any reasonable doubt that the social system of Laissez faire capitalism harmonizes with the requirements of an individual's existence, of your existence.**

Now that you've finished this breathtaking report, you may be wondering if it is possible for you to become a "Master of Human Action."

Here's something to think about. If you master the science of human action would you call yourself a praxeologist. Maybe, maybe not. You know I call myself a praxeologist, although my proclamation might make the great Ludwig von Mises turn in his grave.

Honestly folks, it doesn't matter what you call yourself, as long as you understand these life-changing principles. All that matters is that you effectively apply the important and eternal principles everyday of your life. Hold your head high and act as a warrior acts, with confidence and impeccability. The Libertarian Warrior conquers illusions. He knows that whatever you're seeking is yours for the taking.

Part 2

Conquering

More Economic

Illusions

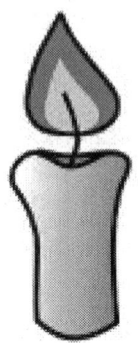

Chapter 1

Government Ought

to

Do Something

Chapter 1

Government Ought to
Do Something

Doesn't it perplex you that people search outside of themselves for answers to life's problems. One of the worse places to seek answers is the government. Of course, greedy, altruistic people promise to supply the solutions. One quick glance at our economic woes tells us this isn't the place to look.

During Ronald Reagan's inaugural address delivered on January 20, 1981, he said "In this present crisis, government is not the solution to our problems: government is the problem. Well, things haven't changed. People still believe in the illusion of government solutions to economic problems.

Let's get real and face reality. Governments are masters at creating poverty, misery, death and destruction. What they are very inept at is creating wealth and prosperity for their citizens. In fact, the only way governments can help economies is by getting the hell out of the way.

The belief that the "Government ought to do something" is not only an illusion, but qualifies as delusional thinking.

Illusion

People act as if the government possesses magical powers that can solve our individual and social ills. All this mythical entity has to do is wave its wand and all our problems vanish in a blink of an eye. I know, most people would state that this belief is ridiculous. However, is that what they really think. I can prove that the majority of people act as if the government somehow acquired omnipotent powers.

How many times have you heard someone say "Government ought to do something." I don't know about you, but I've been hearing that mindless statement all my life. If you ask the person making the statement what government should do, quite often he says he doesn't

41

know—but the government should do something.

When enough people believe in "The Big Illusion" or what some call "The Big Lie" there will always be charlatans that claim to know what should be done. These purveyors of mischief and mayhem usually practice occupations called politician, intellectual, bureaucrat, world-improver, do-gooder, altruist, etc. Government needs the support and propaganda tactics of these "professionals" to endow "The Big Illusion" with a potency of its own. Of course, the establishment media makes sure we have enough deluded citizens waiting in line to receive their shot of the "cure."

What Government is Not

Government is not some real life Santa Claus that dispenses gift upon its citizens, despite the fact that altruists and intellectuals claim otherwise. It may seem government performs magical feats, but this is an illusion of limited consciousness.

Let's continue our attack and conquer "The Big Illusion."

1. As mention before, government has absolutely no earned wealth of its own. It definitely doesn't have the tools to create wealth. The only money it can get its greedy hands on comes from the hapless citizens in the form of taxes and inflation. It also sells bonds on the open market; however, it's apparent that the funds it receives are diverted from productive free enterprise ventures into government coffers.
2. Since it doesn't create any wealth, how can it possibly dispense "goodies" to its citizens? There is only one way. It extracts the "gifts" from its citizens. When the voters support another government program and vote for politicians who "promise" to institute it, they unwittingly confiscate themselves.
3. I think we understand that government masquerades as a Santa Claus figure, but in reality manifests as an evil Robin Hood. Even the supposedly good Robin Hood is a thief. Forcibly taking from one individual or group to give to another individual or group is

immoral, no matter what justification do-gooders and altruists spout to support it.

The Nature of Government

1. Government is the apparatus of violent compulsion and coercion (force). It's only legitimate function is to protect an individual's life, liberty and property. All transfer programs amount to nothing but theft.
2. Two types of exchange between groups and individuals exist, voluntary and involuntary. In a voluntary exchange, all parties enter it of their free will. Government has no business interfering with this type of exchange. In an involuntary exchange, at least one party is involved against his will. Robbery, rape, murder, theft, etc. are examples of involuntary exchanges. Government applies its apparatus of violent compulsion and coercion to arrest criminals involved these anti-social acts. It is government's only legitimate function.
3. When people notice social phenomena they disapprove of—acts that result from voluntary exchanges, they often claim "Government ought to do something." What the man or woman who makes this thoughtless statement needs to realize is that he or she is supporting the use of government force against innocent people. The liberty violator advocates restrictions against individual freedom.

Conclusion

As you can see the statement "government ought to do something" is a dangerous illusion and leads to massive violations of an individual's life, liberty and property. In fact, the disastrous results we are experiencing in the form of economic turmoil, foreign excursions, restrictions on personal freedom, etc. are caused by the growth of that gigantic, destructive entity called "Big Government." Its citizens have allowed a sentence we can call the "The Big Illusion", a simple but dangerous five-word sentence to create a beast of mythical proportions that threatens to permanently destroy "The American Dream." Fortunately, you and I are doing our best to conquer that evil illusion. We live as warriors for personal liberty and freedom.

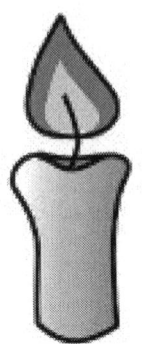

Chapter 2

Psychology of

Government

Interventionism

Chapter 2

Psychology of Government Interventionism

Now that we conquered some economic illusions, let's continue our momentum.

We proved that government solutions to our economic woes would not result in a long-term recovery. Hopefully, you will no longer allow the illusions of the political and financial establishment to influence your personal and financial affairs.

Are you convinced that praxeology, the science of human action conclusively proves that all forms of interference with the marketplace are self-defeating and doomed to failure?

We must face the fact that so-called "intellectuals" continue to be hard-core supporters and initiators of government "solutions" to our economic woes. Tragically, they convinced the masses that government "help" could cure their financial problems. You may wonder why anyone would fall for an obvious illusion.

Let's get into the psychology behind government interventionism.

Envy

The negative emotion of envy plays havoc on a person's peace of mind. Feelings of envy unleashed and put into action negatively affect everyone involved, including the purveyor of discord. When individuals succumb to their negative emotions in personal relationships, they cause themselves and those closest to them much hurt, pain and disharmony. Once government institutionalizes envy in the form of massive spending programs that transfers wealth from the productive to the non-productive, the accelerating social costs begin to destroy the fabric of society.

I certainly understand the negative emotion of envy. Individuals have the unfortunate habit of comparing themselves with others. The envious ones are lead by an external frame of reference instead of a more

47

effective internal frame of reference. So what does the person consumed with envy do? He compares himself unfavorably to "the Jones." How painful it is to see others succeed while the unfortunate person suffers through a life of struggle and want. Sadly, most are unable to look within to discover the root cause of their lack of the good or even necessary things in life. Instead, they search for answers on the outside, seeking scapegoats they can blame for their own deficiencies.

Politicians "earn" their living by playing the game of "switcheroo." In their cannibalistic game of sacrifice, politicians in their favorite disguise as altruists transform victims into victimizers and visa versa, feeding the innocent to the guilty. Unfortunately, for us, unscrupulous politicians find scapegoats, innocent victims they can use as sacrificial fodder in order to satisfy the unearned needs of envious constituents. Honestly, in our world of massive government interventionism, is anyone's life, liberty and property safe from these predators.

Hate

Underlying the negative emotion of envy is entrenched feelings of hate, submerged somewhere below the surface of a person's conscious mind. Usually, the man or woman transforms hate into more socially acceptable emotions such as envy, jealousy, covetousness, etc. For obvious reasons, many people attempt to hide their hatred of everything good, beautiful and sublime. In fact, I doubt if they are consciously aware of it. Let's face it. Most of us aren't introspective enough to come face to face with our inner-ugliness. It's a rare and dangerous bird who actively displays his hatred and wears it as a badge of honor.

Altruists, absolute moralists, do-gooders and world -improvers "sublimate" their hatred into socially acceptable activities that appeal to the envy of the masses. Tragically, it allows them to pretend they are "saviors" of the world, concerned, loving people who only want to help others. And believe me, there are plenty of neurotic, envious people waiting in line to be "helped." What the do-gooders and do-goodies refuse to admit, is that they are causing the rapid decline of Western Civilization.

The End of Government Interventionism

Your mind now perceives that all government interventionism must eventually end, either through the short-term pain of renunciation or the long-term death of our economic system. There are no other possibilities. Tragically, it appears a significant number of Americans have chosen the latter, maybe in a futile attempt to shift the burden to their children and their children's children. Only showing concern for your own irrationally selfish needs and not caring about future generations demonstrates unbridled envy and hate.

I believe irrationally selfish people are in for some unpleasant surprises. The treacherous anti-life philosophy of social altruism and its practice of government interventionism continually sucks the life-blood out of our already fragile economy. It appears as if members of the political and financial establishment won't be able to shift the complete burden of economic decline to future generations. The sad fact is that many innocent, productive people could also face the difficult times that come unbidden with economic chaos.

The Individual Conquers Economic Illusions

An individual who lives impeccably by practicing rational selfishness conquers the forces of economic illusions. Overcoming the illusions and delusions of the political and financial establishment is critical for your continued success.

The Libertarian Warrior doesn't allow social altruists and envious people to sabotage all that is pleasurable, fulfilling and sublime. He captures personal liberty and freedom. Become a warrior and take what is rightfully yours—values you have earned.

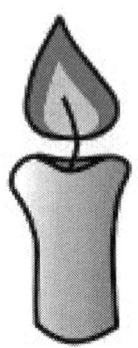

Chapter 3

The Stability Illusion

Chapter 3

The Stability Illusion

Have you noticed our political and financial leaders seem addicted to the notion of stability? Members of this elite group of economic nitwits come up with illusionary schemes for stabilizing the economy. Here's something to consider. If our "beloved" leaders actually achieve stability, progress would be out of the question.

In his masterpiece "Human Action" Ludwig von Mises states "Stability, the establishment of which the program of stabilization aims at, is an empty and contradictory notion. The urge towards action, i.e., improvement in the conditions of life, is inborn in man."

Do you know what should be evident to all? As a human, you change moment to moment. Most of the time the change is imperceptible; other times you experience rapid change. Think back, let's say about 10 years ago. You realize change has been the one constant in your life.

In the sphere of human action only the aprioristic categories of action are eternal, everything else fluctuates. I know change can be hard to accept. We become quite comfortable within our comfort zone—even when it displeases us. Instead of initiating change, we often allow it to batter us with unwelcome surprises.

Let's accept the fact that where there is action, there is change. You cannot exist without change. Maybe you dream about existing in a utopia, a heaven where everything remains the same. You never have to face the unpleasantness of uncertainty again. All your pleasures, dreams and desires happily repeat through eternity.

Remember the old Talking Heads song "Heaven"

"Everyone is trying to get to the bar.
The name of the bar, the bar is called heaven.
The band in Heaven they play my favorite song.
They play it one more time, they play it all night long.

Oh heaven, heaven is a place where nothing, nothing ever happens.
Heaven is a place where nothing, nothing ever happens."

Now that's what I call a profound song, one that reveals an eternal truth. Plus, it's great music.

You're probably familiar with index numbers. The government supplies us with numbers that are supposed to inform us about price changes. Unfortunately, we suffer the prospect of government bureaucrats deciding what to include in their basket of goods and services. You can imagine how easily it is for them to manipulate the index for the benefit of government—and special interests that rely on government interventionism.

Do you see the flaw in their reasoning? Index numbers only indicate a state of rest at a certain point in time, revealing nothing about changing consumer desires and the entrepreneurial activities that create price changes. In all honesty, judicious shoppers know more about changing prices than government economists. Do you allow index numbers to influence your behavior?

Every action you embark on initiates change. Stability is nothing but an illusion. Can you imagine reading a history book and the facts of the 19th and 20th centuries are identical. Why the whole idea appears ludicrous—except maybe to a politically correct revisionist historian. You're probably thinking it's beyond the power of governments to bring change to a standstill and usher in an era of stability.

Can you imagine people suddenly waking up tomorrow morning and deciding they no longer desire improvement in their lives. Let's fantasize for a moment. Our political and financial leaders suddenly determine there's no room for social or economic improvement, deciding to leave things alone. Now that would be heaven!

The Federal Reserve System claims it exists to stabilize the currency. Yeah, sure. Since it's creation in 1913, the dollar has lost more than 95% of its value. Anyway, the idea of stability crumbles as an illusion of limited consciousness.

Once again, I'm quoting from Ludwig von Mises' "Human Action." "What economic calculation requires is a monetary system whose functioning is not sabotaged by government interference." We can accomplish that goal by adopting a 100% Gold Standard—and by abolishing the Federal Reserve System.

Here's the bottom line. The notion of a government created economy of stability and prosperity is contradictory and unrealizable, because it defies all logic and reason.

Individuals acting in their best interest by engaging in value for value relationships create positive and rewarding change. Stability in human action is equivalent to the existence of a rock or maybe it's more accurate to state, stability equals death. Isn't it fun conquering illusions!

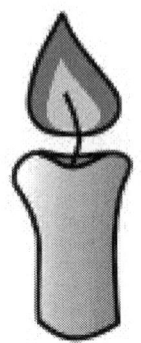

Chapter 4

The Failure of

Government

Interventionism

Chapter 4

The Failure of Government Interventionism

During an economic crisis, you can almost hear the cries of panic and despair. If you listen closely, you overhear desperate statements such as: Government must do something to solve our economic woes. It must rescue Wall Street. It can't let the banking system go belly-up. Please do something to save our housing market. You must save capitalism from the effects of capitalism—even if it takes an injection of trillions of dollars. Oh beloved representatives of government, great masters of finance, have mercy on our pocketbooks and standard of living. Well, maybe we didn't actually hear that last statement.

What many people do not realize is that the government, with the assistance of the Federal Reserve System, creates our economic problems. Asking political and financial leaders to solve an economic crisis is the same as hiring a fox to guard the hen house.

Government and the Federal Reserve System

Let's go back a century and trace the destruction of our economic system. In the year 1913, it received a double-whammy. Special interests began the expropriation of the American citizen with the Federal Reserve System and the Federal Income Tax.

Did you know that on May 20, 1895 the Supreme Court declared a Federal Income Tax unconstitutional. Of course, liberty violators never give up their efforts to plunder productive citizens. In February 1913, the Federal Income Tax was ratified. It levied a 1% tax on all incomes over $3000, and a progressive surtax on all incomes over $20,000. Interventionists, do-gooders and altruists praised it. In fact, along with the Federal Reserve System, it was the first step toward a complete confiscation of private property—a liberty violator's dream come true.

The Federal Reserve System allowed government spending to soar to the stratosphere. It also enabled the political and financial establishment to create artificial booms. I'm sure you're perceptive enough to know that all artificial booms end in busts.

The Fed creates a boom by increasing the money supply through the means of artificially lowering the rate of interest. Isn't it evident that the manipulated interest rate supplies false information. Like a ship crossing treacherous waters without a compass, individuals attempt to make correct entrepreneurial and investment decisions without the compass of a correct interest rate.

Interest rate manipulation reduces the effectiveness of entrepreneurs and investors. Incredibly, some believe that the false rates assist them in anticipating future market changes more accurately. I guess we had better conquer another illusion.

In the book "Theory of Money and Credit" Ludwig von Mises demonstrates how central banks create "phony" money by artificially lowering interest rates. Unfortunately, interest rate manipulation causes some entrepreneurs to make uneconomic investments, what Mises calls malinvestments. What is unprofitable at the market rate of interest suddenly looks profitable at an artificially lower rate. The illusion of profits jump kicks a boom cycle. At first, business pick ups, workers are hired, the capital goods industry booms and overall prices begin to rise. Hey, it's party time.

Let's move further down the thorny path of an illusion. Eventually the boom must end. Oops, the party comes to a crashing end. We've seen it many times with the great depression of the 30's, the tech boom, the housing boom, etc.; and we will see it again as long as the Federal Reserve System continues to try holding interest rates below their natural rate.

Here's the way the boom ends in a bust. Unsound entrepreneurial ventures prove unprofitable, resulting in business failure, unemployment and general economic malaise. Sadly, we have the Fed attempting to prop up the economy with stimulus programs referred to as quantitative easing (QE), which is just another term for inflation. Now that's a solution, cure inflation with more inflation. By the way, that is why we haven't experienced a strong recovery. The Fed actually prevents the economy from recovering with interest rates close to 'gasp' 0%. Are you satisfied with the rate of return on your savings account? I call the Fed's monetary policy quack quantitative easing (QQE).

We live in an age where the new religion of our era is faith in the "healing" power of the government. When the economy begins reeling, the citizens call for more government healing. Now, that's what we can call a gigantic illusion.

The Entitlement Mentality – We Want It Now

Economic Law (Praxeology) conclusively proves that all government interference with voluntary exchanges fail, and will only worsen the situation. Why do people support ill-advised social policies that are detrimental to their long-term well-being? Apparently, a significant amount of men and women suffer from a short-term mentality. We can admit that it's perfectly normal to prefer now to later. However, it's irrationally selfish to disregard the intermediate and long-term consequences of your actions. The entitlement mentality causes people to consume the seed corn of progress. Do you understand why humongous personal and social debt plagues our once great nation? We all know the national debt soars out of control—at least I hope we know.

The rationally selfish individual considers all the consequences of his actions. He enjoys life today, but makes sure there is something left for the future. The irrationally selfish person wants immediate gratification, even it doesn't leave anything for tomorrow.

Hail! Hail! Unhampered Capitalism

One of the legendary pioneers of Rock 'n' Roll, Chuck Berry sang the song "School Day." In a famous exciting verse, he sings "Hail, Hail rock and roll. Deliver me from the days of old. Long live rock and roll." My sentiments exactly.

I say Hail! Hail! Unhampered Capitalism." You know, capitalism delivered the masses from the days of old, the days of poverty and destitution, and filled their horn of plenty with an abundance of goods and services. Unfortunately, we've never experienced the marvels of unhampered capitalism. Governments and special interests have sabotaged it from the start with destructive schemes of government interventionism and numerous variations of the anti-life social system, socialism.

Capitalism supplies the goods and services men and women require for a uniquely human existence, and it does the job quite generously. All other social systems thwart the effort of the individual to provide for the requirements of his life. So once again, let's shout Hail! Hail! Unhampered Capitalism. Long live unhampered capitalism. If you prefer silent power, feel it in your body, mind and spirit.

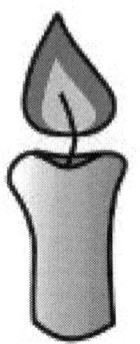

Chapter 5

The American

Dream - Illusion or

Possibility

Chapter 5

The American Dream – Illusion or Possibility

More than 30 years ago, Robert Ringer wrote the classic book "Restoring the American Dream." Ringer's monumental book caused quite a sensation, soaring to Number 1 on the New York Times bestseller list. Along with some other libertarian classics, his book paved the way for the "liberal" massacre in the 1980 election. The voters wisely removed some big spending anti-capitalists from office. Certainly, a new era of free enterprise and liberty was within our reach. We would render big government obsolete.

Now we are well into the 21st century. What happened to the elegant and logical dreams of the lovers of personal liberty and freedom? Sure, libertarians and members of the Tea Party put up a courageous fight. Despite their efforts, big government continues to grow out of control.

Let's face another harsh reality. Members of the political and financial establishment nourish their corrupted souls by violating personal liberty and freedom and wrecking economic systems. Do you know that we jail more people than countries run by the bloodiest despots—with the perpetrators of injustice making sure that around 75% of those incarcerated are for victimless crimes.

You've got to wonder. What happened to the marvelous vision of liberty and freedom our founding fathers so richly bestowed on us. Why must we suffer the sorry consequences caused by a government on the road to ruin.

Here's the bottom line. We must get to the root of the matter if we have any chance of Restoring the American Dream.

Natural Law

According to Natural Law, an individual has a right to his life, liberty and property. He owns his life and the fruits of his labor. Nobody possesses the right to expropriate these by force—and that includes the method of seizure called "will of the majority."

We can also conclude that an individual has the right to engage in any voluntary exchange without interference from the government. He owns his life and body, so he can consume any substance of his choice.

Here's something to think about. Altruists preach the anti-life philosophy of self-sacrifice and self-denial, attempting to sacrifice the lone individual for "the good of society." The anti-concept of selflessness is irrational and contradictory, flagrantly violating Natural Law. Since it defies reason and logic, altruists, do-gooders and world-improvers enlist the violent compulsion and coercion of the government to force this evil on hapless citizens.

Consistent violations of Natural Law eat away at individual rights, systematically destroying the American Dream.

Economic Law

Economic Law starts it chain of reasoning with basic premises that are self-evident. We call these premises 'a priori' principles. Praxeology (Human Action) is the deductive science that deals with Economic Law. Altruists and other liberty violators claim there is no exact science of economics. Fortunately, we conquered that illusion in an earlier chapter. The denial of the laws of economics gives them the license to adopt the idea that anything goes. And anything goes—in the form of extreme violations of Economic Law.

I shouldn't have to inform you that our economic system is rift with these violations. The government continues to inflict irreparable damage on the marketplace. If you or I violate the laws of economics, we must pay the piper. Members of the establishment use political power to make sure they are granted immunity from the justice the marketplace imposes on violators of Economic Law.

How do speculators make money? By successfully directing capital investment. Well, how do entrepreneurs earn profits? Successfully organizing and directing production. Who should be producing goods and services? Obviously, the most efficient producers in their role of satisfying the consumers' most urgent desires. All must anticipate future change quicker than competitors in order to profit.

OK, how does the government "make" money? By taking its citizens' money through taxes, inflation and onerous regulations.

When the government blatantly violates the laws of economics, the marketplace attempts to dish out the necessary penalties. Regrettably for us, government has the power to tax and inflate, weapons it uses with reckless abandon, extending their deplorable violations of Economic Law.

We all know about the bailouts, which only benefited members of the political and financial establishment. However, do you realize the long-term damage quack quantitative easing (QQE) will cause to our already fragile economic system? The Fed's unsound monetary interventions will eventually result in consequences that damage innocent people. One of the dire outcomes is the elimination of savings and investment, the only method of creating wealth and prosperity. The average citizen finds it almost impossible to accumulate capital when he receives a miniscule rate of near 0% on his savings account. What a swindle!

Diagnosis

Here's a diagnosis of what causes the destruction of the American Dream.

The political and financial establishment's disregard of Economic Law results in massive violations of the individual's life, liberty and property. It makes you wonder how many of these perpetrators of injustice purposely violate your rights.

Sadly, the deluded masses support government interventionism, impervious to the fact that the policies instituted are not in their best interest. Irrationally selfish people line up at the government smorgasbord of benefits, unconcerned that the productive members of society must pick up the tab. Since these people live in a world of illusion, the short-term mentality disease plagues them. One of these days, the piper will demand payment for their refusal to acknowledge reality. Remember, the government earns no wealth of its own. It can only obtain it through the efforts of people who produce wealth. The irrationally selfish, along with members of the establishment eventually suck most of the wealth out of the economy. We can hope that enough rationally selfish individuals survive to pick up the pieces.

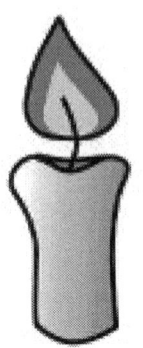

Chapter 6

The American

Dream - Illusion or

Possibility - Part 2

Chapter 6

The American Dream – Illusion or Possibility – Part 2

In Part 1, we diagnosed the destruction of the American Dream by exposing shameless governmental violations of Natural and Economic Law. What's disturbing is that the majority of people support the transgressions, unwittingly helping the government lead us down the road to ruin.

The Constitution and Individual Rights

You probably already know the government reigns supreme as earth's most malicious violator of an individual's life, liberty and property. Common crooks look like boy scouts or alter boys compared with this entity of violent compulsion and coercion. As you continue reading, you will discover solutions that can prevent and stop its attacks on our God-given rights.

Some libertarians advocate eliminating the institution of government. Murray Rothbard's book "For a New Liberty – The Libertarian Manifesto" and Morris and Linda Tennehill's book "The Market for Liberty" presents some cogent and interesting ideas. For our purposes, we are assuming a strictly limited government, although I wonder if any government qualifies to run even the dog-catching service.

The Constitution must explicitly forbid Federal, State and Local governments from interfering with the voluntary exchanges of its citizens—and any consumption of goods and services that result from the exchanges. Now, that's what we can call plain and simple. Laissez faire (unhampered) capitalism is the only social system in harmony with this constitutional amendment.

We must prevent the government from violating Natural and Economic Law. Government exists for one purpose only; to protect the individual's life, liberty and property. Our founding fathers marvelous

67

achievement was The Declaration of Independence. The sorry state of affairs created by our government would send them into a condition of apoplexy.

Eliminating Government Agencies

We must abolish most governmental agencies because their existence violates Natural and Economic Law. The logical course of action requires eliminating FCC, FAA, OSHA, FDA, EPA, SEC and other agencies to numerous to mention. By time you read this, some of these might have changed their name. The above mentioned agencies commit gross violations of individual rights. For instance, the DEA (Drug Enforcement Agency) and its supporters completely disregard individual rights. Just as prohibition was doomed to failure, so is the war on drugs.

The Federal Reserve System

The Federal Reserve System manifests as an engine of monetary mayhem that we can happily abolish. Its inflationary policies trigger most of our economic catastrophes. Sustained inflationary measures cause boom and bust cycles and eventual monetary collapse. **The Fed benefits the elite, members of the political and financial establishment, at the expense of the rest of us.** It destroys the savings of hard-working Americans with its legalized theft.

Here's an idea we can toss around. Let's consider the 100% Gold Standard. Politicians cannot manipulate the quantity of gold as they manipulate the supply of paper money. Gold is scarce; only productive effort in the form of mining can produce it. On the other hand, fiat currency can be increased willy-nilly, which is why the paper money system is a disaster. Remember the 5-cent coke or gas at 25 cents per gallon. We know who benefits from the Fed's monetary policies and it isn't us.

We can conclude that the Gold Standard prevents monetary inflation, allowing wealth producers to retain their earnings. The 100% Gold

Standard cures many of our economic woes, such as rising prices and the chaos caused by boom and bust cycles.

Taxes

You no doubt feel the pain from discriminatory taxation. Most taxation is an outright theft of the individual's life and productive effort. You can make a case we need a minimum tax for the protection of an individual's life, liberty and property.

Government transfer programs equal theft. No amount of justification from altruists, do-gooders and world-improvers for taking from Peter to give to Paul can refute this basic fact. Platitudes such as "the good of society", "for the commonweal" and "from each according to his ability to each according to his need" are illogical and irrelevant. It doesn't matter what euphemism a person uses to justify confiscatory taxation. Theft is theft. Dishonesty is dishonesty. A=A. Of course, if you believe in the doublespeak of George Orwell's book "1984", then you could rationalize that theft is voluntary giving, dishonesty is truthfulness and A=B.

The power to tax—and inflate the currency is the power to destroy. I don't believe we can allow the government to wield these massive weapons of destruction.

The Night Watchman

Government should serve the same function as the night watchman at a factory. Another comparison is it should play the same role as the "Maytag Man"; you know, nothing to do. Imagine reducing government to a minimum function. Allow your imagination to travel to the glorious days when everyone's life, liberty and property becomes off-limits from the predatory practices of altruists, politicians and bureaucrats.

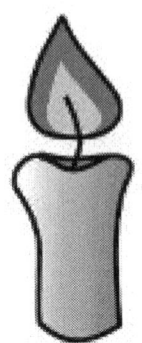

Chapter 7

The American

Dream - Illusion or

Possibility - Part 3

Chapter 7

The American Dream – Illusion or Possibility – Part 3

Only one social system protects an individual's life, liberty and property, unhampered capitalism (free enterprise). Here's a system that corresponds to Natural and Economic Law.

Government interventionism tramples on individual rights. Any interference with voluntary exchanges violates Natural and Economic Law. Government exists for one purpose and one purpose only, to protect the individual's life, liberty and property. If it performed its function correctly, it would protect individual rights by enforcing objective laws against involuntary exchanges (criminal activities).

How do we relegate government to its only legitimate function—and how do we get from heavy-handed interventionism to unhampered capitalism?

Here are three possible solutions.

The Immediate Solution

Certainly, it's immoral for someone to live at the expense of another. Government policies institutionalize the anti-life philosophy of altruism. Let's move forward to permanently protecting individual rights.

Imagine what it would be like if we eliminated all government agencies that do not exist for the protection of life, liberty and private property. Smile, as you see each agency that interferes with voluntary exchanges fading away.

Both the Federal Income Tax and the Federal Reserve System become history. We say goodbye to the confiscatory taxes and inflationary money that plunder productive citizens.

Here's something that might be hard to accept. Unemployment insurance, minimum wage laws, food stamps, corporate welfare, anti-trust laws, etc. will have to go. Nobody has the right to live at the expense of others. It's an illusion to think the government possesses any earned wealth. We eliminate all transfer programs. Stealing from productive citizens to give to others is wrong.

We must immediately repeal all victimless crime laws, releasing from prison all offenders jailed for these so-called offenses. Prosecutors will drop any pending victimless crime cases. Believe it or not, this alone should eliminate at least 75% of property crimes.

Government will relinquish its control over our road system. Any business that results in the death of more than 30,000 customers per year is highly inefficient. Private ownership of the road system is the only viable alternative. Free enterprise is without exception more efficient than government bureaucracy is.

Private firms can handle all voluntary transactions—and that includes the mail service currently mishandled by the postal system. As the service goes down, down, down—the cost of a stamp goes up, up, up.

Government will no longer interfere or prohibit voluntary exchanges —or any consumption of goods that result from these exchanges. An individual owns his life and body—and this is irrevocable.

The 5% Solution

You are intelligent enough to know that the above logical and moral solution is politically unacceptable to the vast majority of people. I admit that you might feel uncomfortable with it. We need to acknowledge that many citizens are dependent on the government for their very survival. Altruists, do-gooders and world-improvers did everything possible to turn people in helpless children. Plus, the political and financial establishment swindled them with their spurious monetary escapades.

Let's ask some tough questions. How would an eighty year-old senior citizen survive when his only source of income is his Social Security check. How would elderly and handicapped people receive medical care in the short-term if suddenly their Medicare and Medicaid benefits vanished. I believe in the power of charities, but it will take some time for these to prosper; especially since members of the political and financial establishment pulled one of the greatest heists of its citizens' wealth in the history of mankind. You probably notice the deductions from your payroll for Social Security and Medicare.

I will state outright that nobody have no right to live at the expense of others. Tragically, our "beloved" political and social leaders convinced them otherwise; leading hapless citizens to the illusion of the entitlement mentality.

Politicians, social altruists, do-gooders and world-improvers created a banquet consisting of a free lunch. The mass media did their part by feeding people enormous amounts of propaganda that conned the unwary and the irrationally selfish individual into believing that government handouts pointed the way to prosperity and independence. Little did he or she know the payment for unearned benefits was his or her freedom and self-reliance. The piper always demands payment.

Now, you might tell me these people have minds of their own and could have resisted the barrage of lies and misinformation. I agree. It would make life easier if they exercised their reasoning abilities and resisted the half-truths and lies altruists feed them.

Sadly, only a small percentage of people have cultivated the ability to think independently and creatively. The Fed's artificial booms have tricked even some independent thinkers.

Although, I'm not entirely happy to present the 5% solution, I believe it constitutes a vast improvement over current conditions. Still, people need to learn that theft is theft, even when altruists claim it's for a good cause.

Some of the measures presented as immediate solutions remain necessary, such as the repeal of all victimless crime laws. These liberty violations must immediately cease. We also abolish the Federal Reserve System. A 100% Gold Standard replaces the Fed.

Here's the 5% solution.

We reduce all government spending by 5% each month. We also reduce the Federal Income Tax with the 5% solution. Eventually, if a minimum tax is required to support the government's only function of protecting an individual's life, liberty and property it will have to be less than 5%, and that needs to be carefully scrutinized. The goal of any libertarian is to eventually abolish all taxes.

Here's an example of the 5% solution. If a person receives let's say

$1000 per month, his payment would be reduced $50 per month over a 20 month period; giving him a chance to adjust to the new situation.

We may have to supply social security benefits to the elderly for the rest of their lives. Some can no longer take care of themselves. We know that no one has a right to live at the expense of another. However, the political establishment pilfered the social security money we paid into the system. There's nothing left. Here's a novel ideal. Maybe—only altruists, do-gooders, world-improvers, absolute moralists, politicians, bureaucrats and their supporters should bear the burden of support.

The renaissance of personal and economic freedom will definitely ignite an economic boom, one based on real wealth and increased productivity. The unleashing of unhampered capitalism results in charities thriving, which could render the social security system obsolete.

Picture this. We finally experience an era of prosperity and abundance that is almost unimaginable under current circumstances. In addition, the government finally withers away.

The 1% Solution

We would resort to all the above measures, but at a rate of 1% per month. The main advantage is that it gives people more time to adjust by removing some of the pressure and discomfort they may experience.

You are probably thinking that the major disadvantage is the fact that we have to trust the government to honor the program for the eight years and four months it would take to complete it. It's difficult to keep an establishment politician honest for even one day. In addition, special interest groups would apply political pressure for "special" exceptions. We know that exceptions usually become the rule.

I feel uneasy about anyone living at the expense of another—even if it is for only one second. Coveting and stealing is immoral. Still, the 1% solution would be considerably better than what currently plagues us.

Conclusion

I am a positive thinker who believes individuals possess the power to overcome adversity. The impeccable warrior discovers practical and spiritual solutions to life's problems. He conquers his illusions.

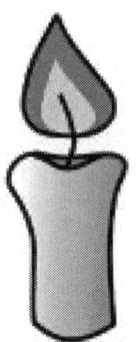

Chapter 8

Libertarianism

Illusion or Solution

Chapter 8

Libertarianism – Illusion or Solution

Now I would like you to experience hope for the future. First, you must allow yourself to open up your imagination and consider the following.

Have you noticed that when people discuss political and social issues they act as if they base their opinions on unalterable facts, even though they completely disregard Natural and Economic Law. Politicians are especially adept at truth-twisting and making illogic sound logical. Logical thinkers and lovers of liberty and freedom face a tragic comedy of illusions becoming socially acceptable—and the law of the land.

Let's define opinion. According to The Free Dictionary, an opinion is "a belief or conclusion held with confidence but not substantiated by positive knowledge or proof."

Subjectivity

Unquestionably, there is nothing wrong with possessing opinions. If you didn't have them, you couldn't make decisions. Imagine attempting to decide what you desire or don't desire without opinions to guide you. Preferring A to B and B to C is perfectly natural.

Now altruists, politicians and world-improvers may find it difficult to accept that you have preferences. After all, these violators of individual rights seem to be afflicted with a disease called "control freakitis."

All your preferences, including the music you love, the food you prefer to consume, what beverages satisfy your thirst, the clothes you adorn, and what movies you like, are completely subjective. We cannot measure your values, although establishment economists attempt this impossible feat.

Natural Law, Economic Law and Opinions

Here's something important to ponder. Problems arise when an individual's opinion violates Natural and Economic Law. Unfounded opinions create most of the world's problems. I'm sure you noticed they also cause individuals much mischief in their personal affairs. Have you ever argued with someone over an obvious false statement or belief?

Here's the scoop on Natural Law.

As mentioned before, an individual has a right to his life, liberty and property. He owns his life and the fruits of his labor. Any aggression committed against him violates this law and is therefore criminal. Social systems that continually violate Natural Law include communism, socialism, fascism, Nazism and big government interventionism. What the uninitiated person fails to realize is the above social systems prey on individual rights. These systems fail miserably because each one violates Natural Law.

How about Economic Law?

Do you wonder why harmony and well-being seems absent from our economic system? Wonder no more. Our political and financial leaders act as if Economic Law doesn't exist. In fact, we conquered their anti-economic beliefs many times. Every page of this book accomplished its mission.

We demonstrated that Economic Law begins reasoning with 'a priori' principles, which makes it a deductive system. It manifests as the exciting science of praxeology (human action). Establishment economists only care about aggregates, completely ignoring the individual. Praxeology deals with the actions of individuals, the actions of you and me.

The Objective System – Libertarianism

Do you know that Libertarianism is an objective system based on Natural and Economic Law? Happily, it supports the individual's right to his life, liberty and property.

Do you love personal and economic freedom? You'll be thrilled to know that a libertarian social system guarantees no one becomes a slave to another and no one has the right to expropriate the fruits of your labor. We can emphatically state that it's immoral to live at someone's expense. When the government institutes the anti-life social beliefs of altruists, do-gooders and world-improvers, it far exceeds the hostile actions of common criminals.

With certainty, we can state that Economic Law proves all forms of governmental interference with individuals indulging in voluntary exchanges causes unfortunate consequences.

Let's face it. Members of the political and financial establishment are intent on destroying the hopes, dreams and desires of the innocent, of the producer, of the hardworking American. Make no mistake about it. All forms of socialism and government interventionism violate Natural and Economic Law. These enforce the spurious doctrine of "from each according to his ability, to each according to his need." I think we can agree that that pretty much describes theft on a grand scale.

Here's another insight for you. Economic calculation becomes impossible under a pure system of socialism. You can't have market prices if you abolish markets. By the way, communism is socialism. Anyway, when the government restricts the free flow of information between individuals, it severely hampers the operation of the social system. The fact that a socialist government attempts to control everything through central planning is enough to permanently cripple productivity and well-being.

Does it infuriate you to know that this is what our political and financial leaders want for our once great country? These creators of mischief and mayhem desire complete control over your life and money.

Libertarianism

I'm proud to state that Libertarianism advocates unhampered capitalism (free enterprise), a social system that completely corresponds to the laws of economics (praxeology). You've got to marvel about how it harmonizes with Natural Law. Yes! Here is an objective social system.

You know, when a libertarian defends this system by using the principles of Natural and Economic Law, his statements are in tune with reality, and we cannot consider them unfounded opinions.

Conclusion

By now, I hope you realize Libertarianism is a viable social system that can free us from troubled times. It's definitely not based on floating abstractions, unfounded opinions. It manifests as an objective system based on the laws of the universe.

The Author — Robert Meyer

Robert Meyer is the author of "7 Powerful Steps for Conquering Life's Illusions." He was born in Cincinnati, Ohio. He possesses an extensive background in many areas. For 35 years, he has studied economics, philosophy, psychology and metaphysics, integrating these disciplines into a coherent philosophy of life. For more than 23 years, he has indulged in meditation practices to increase his power of reason and help him reach expanded states of awareness. His sales career also helped give him a deeper understanding of human nature.

He realizes there are basic principles of Human Action that will help people become successful at achieving their goals and desires. His knowledge that life is to be lived on a physical, emotional, mental and spiritual level allowed him to discover "Way of the Libertarian Warrior." He lives in Garland, Texas.

For more information visit his blog: Way of the Libertarian Warrior and visit his website: The Libertarian Way

Made in the USA
San Bernardino, CA
19 January 2016